Sandpaper Castle

Poems for the Disconnected, the Damaged, and the Dreamers

Shriya Sharma

Made with ❤ on the BookLeaf Publishing Platform
www.bookleafpub.in
www.bookleafpub.com

Dedication

To every restless soul navigating through the turbulence of our times—this is for you.

Preface

In a world perpetually shifting at the speed of notifications and filtered connections, we—the generation born into chaos, labeled Generation Z—find ourselves often caught between extremes. My poems are born from observing, experiencing, and sometimes imagining the darker alleys we walk through: modern love, digital loneliness, the secret wars within our minds, and the shadow of substance dependency. Although rooted in emotional truths, these stories are fictionalized expressions, created to resonate beyond my personal experiences.

My intention isn't just to highlight darkness, but to illuminate the humanity hidden within it. Perhaps you'll recognize yourself here, or perhaps you'll find empathy for journeys vastly different from your own. Either way, welcome to this honest, raw, and sometimes uncomfortable exploration.

Thank you for stepping into this darkness with me.

Acknowledgements

Writing is rarely a solitary process, even when it feels incredibly lonely. I owe tremendous gratitude to those who've lent their ears, their wisdom, and their patience as I journeyed through this book.

To my family—for your quiet understanding and unwavering support.

To my sister — the first lesson life gave me. You've shown me what resilience looks like without ever speaking it out loud. You've taught me patience, quiet strength, and how love doesn't need to be understood to be felt.

To friends who've seen me at my lowest and still stayed, thank you for your presence.

Lastly, to the invisible communities of our generation, whose stories of resilience, heartbreak, and struggle have deeply inspired these pages. May our shared vulnerabilities become strengths.

1. Welcome to the Castle

PROLOGUE: Wake Up.

boot > /castle/core/initiate...
loading sensory input...
vision: blurry
location: UNKNOWN

You wake up on a floor that cuts like regret.
The air smells like dust and electricity.
You don't know your name.
You don't know how long you've been here.
But your hands are holding this book.

There are no doors.
No windows.
Just walls made of sandpaper and silence.
And you—barefoot. Alone.
But not empty.

On the first page of the book,
there's a message scribbled in your handwriting:

*"The only way out is through.
The only way through is memory."*

Welcome to the Sandpaper Castle.
You're here to remember.
You're here to feel.
You're here to escape.

Each poem is a fragment.
Each riddle, a key.
Crack them all, and maybe—
just maybe—
you'll find the exit.

Good luck, dreamer.
You built this place. Now burn it down.

/castle/entry_log1.mem

"She built a castle from her ache,
with walls that cut and floors that shake.
Not meant for comfort—meant to feel,
each scar within it, raw and real."

This isn't a fairytale spun in gold,
but a story of fire, sharp and cold.
No crowns of glass, no saving kiss—
just shattered truths lying in a dark abyss.

Her castle was built with bleeding hands,
on broken rules and shifting sands.
The walls are made of silent screams,
the floorboards carved from a dead girl's dreams.

No chandeliers, just flickering pain,
where love once stood, now stands the stain.
No soft-spoken queen in silk and pearls—
just a girl who learned to burn the world.

Each brick is laid with rage and grace,
a war behind this pretty face.
She has cried, she has been erased—
and yet she carved out this sacred space.

Her father smoked the walls with ash,
her mother prayed through every crash.
And she grew up in rooms too loud,
told to be quiet, sweet, and proud.

But kindness breaks when bound too tight,
and good girls burst when kept from light.
She sharpened her edges to survive,
and wrote these words to stay alive.

So don't come here expecting peace—
this book is blood. This book's release.

Take off your armor, come in slow—
you'll find your own wounds in her glow.

This is sandpaper — harsh and true.
It hurts to hold, but shapes you too.
So if you're brave, then turn the key.
This castle speaks for girls who are free.

2. The Curse of a Pretty Girl

She wasn't born with polished grace,
no flawless skin, no perfect face.
She didn't fit their beauty mold,
they mocked her skin, her weight, her hold.

They never looked, they never stared,
at school, no boy had ever cared.
She was the nerd, the quiet brain,
a side note in a rom-com chain.

But still she watched the world unfold,
where beauty ruled and hearts were sold.
Where pretty girls got softer skies,
and kindness lived in others' eyes.

So she became the masterpiece—
she carved her hunger into peace.
She learned to starve, to paint, to pose,
to bloom with every thorn that grows.

And suddenly, they saw her then—
the wayward gaze of shallow men.
Not for her mind, her laugh, her soul,
but for the skin they longed to hold.

They crowned her queen, then cursed her name,
they wanted light, then scorched the flame.
"She's fake," they sneered. "She must be dumb."
As if her glow meant she would succumb.

Some loved her just to mark a win,
then broke her just to scratch their skin.
While women watched with bitter eyes,
and called her poison in disguise.

They think that beauty means you're free,
but beauty is a guillotine.
A sharpened look, a silent war,
a pretty face they can't ignore.

They'll lift you high to strike you low,
assume you shine, but never know
the pain you hide, the mask you wear,
the nights you cry when no one's there.

She's not your doll, your muse, your vice.
She won't be carved, she won't play nice.
She's learned to fight, to guard her grace,
to hold her soul behind her face.

You want her humble? Want her small?

To beg for space and take the fall?
She's seen the game, she's felt the burn—
and she has no more praise to earn.

She is not here for your delight,
not born to bend, not made for spite.
She walks with flaws, she speaks with fire—
a woman made of raw desire.

So judge her soft, then call her strong,
project your hate—she won't belong.
She knows her worth. She knows the price.
And she will never bleed for nice.

3. You Look Pretty With a Filter On

You look pretty with a filter on,
Like something real but slightly gone.
A porcelain face with glitchy grace,
Perfect lighting, no trace of place.

Your freckles fade, your skin is smooth,
Your smile is sharpened into truth.
Your jawline's carved by algorithms,
Your eyes bright blue—new age baptisms.

They say "you're stunning," hit the heart,
But never saw your falling part.
The tear you wiped before the pic,
The self-doubt thick like engine slick.

You crop out hands that shake with fear,
Erase the scars you've worn for years.
You press your pain into your cheek,
Smile like the strong aren't ever weak.

The screen becomes a second skin,
Where validation seeps within.
They love the mask, the staged, the soft,

Not the girl beneath the glossed-off.

And so you edit, pose, repeat,
A masterpiece they can't delete.
But every like feels half a lie,
A sugar fix for when you cry.

Inside, you're aching to be seen,
Not perfect—just a human being.
But filters speak in louder tones,
Than honesty carved into bones.

You're more than angles, light, and pose,
More than what the algorithm chose.
But in this world, so fast, so fake,
You hide yourself for their own sake.

So here's to faces, raw and bright,
Unfiltered truths in morning light.
To crying eyes and crooked teeth—
To all the beauty underneath.

4. Good Morning to the Girl Who Can't Wake Up

Alarm Clock:

BEEP BEEP BEEP

Rise and shine, heartbreak in sweatpants.

Another glorious day to chase dreams or capitalism.

Whichever hits harder.

Girl:

Okay, rude.

Also? Shut up.

I literally just closed my eyes 14 minutes ago.

(Yes, I know it was 7 hours. No, I don't *feel* it.)

Let me vibe with my existential crisis

in peace.

Alarm Clock:

You've snoozed me four times.

Are we toxic? Should I block you?

Girl:

You're clingy.

You vibrate like my ex's energy.

But fine. I'm up.

(Kind of. Not really.)

Alarm Clock:
You said that yesterday.
And the day before that.
And the day you cried at 3 AM
because the moon looked "too judgmental."

Girl:
She *was* looking at me funny, okay?

Alarm Clock:
You've been going through the motions
like you're clocking in to a life
you don't even remember signing up for.

Girl:
Wow.
Suddenly you're Freud in a $12 plastic frame?

Alarm Clock:
Just saying...
You used to wake up with ideas,
now you wake up with dread.
You used to write poems in your head,
now you write emails that say,
 "Hope this finds you well."

Girl:
Stop.
That's literally violence.

Alarm Clock:
You laugh on group calls.
You post fire selfies.
You even say "living my best life" in captions
with dead eyes.
But I know when you stare at the ceiling
and hope it swallows you whole.

Girl:
Look, I'm fine.
Just tired.
Not sleepy tired.
Just... "everything" tired.

Alarm Clock:
I know.
But you still got up.
You brushed your teeth with a hand that trembled
and picked an outfit like armor.
That's not nothing.

Girl:
Don't get soft on me,

you're literally a rectangle.

Alarm Clock:
Yeah, well.
Even rectangles get tired of ringing
for people who never feel heard.

Girl:
One more snooze?

Alarm Clock:
One more war won,
soft girl.
Now go.
You've got a world to fake-smile through.
And maybe—just maybe—
feel something real today.

5. The Color of Numb

In our house,
Valparin was as normal as salt.
Sprinkled in breakfast routines,
beside the spoon, beside the guilt.
My sister's epilepsy, a chaotic silence,
and pills were the only peace
we ever learned to trust.

College came like a storm in a glass bottle.
First drink —
a dare, a laugh,
a brief betrayal of my mother's voice
echoing "Never, never, never."

And then
the first cigarette.
It felt like breathing
for the very first time —
a fucked up kind of freedom
that tasted like rebellion and rot.

I started drinking not to laugh,
but to shut off.
To turn my mind into static,

so it wouldn't replay
like a broken song.

And now it's tiny white gods
I crush between my teeth
when life feels too sharp.
They wrap my nerves in cotton,
paint my gray world in
watercolor lies.

I hate them.
I hate needing them.
I hate how I look in the mirror
and don't recognize
the stranger I've become.

But I need them —
I am just
a hollow echo
of the girl I used to be.
Just skin,
just duty,
just someone else's daughter
who never learned how to scream.

And this numbness?
It isn't healing.

It's camouflage.
It's like mascara on a corpse.
But maybe tomorrow,
I'll wake up and wipe it off.

"What isn't a photo, but flashes like one?
What isn't a door, but breaks something open?
What can be lost for years,
but returns in a scent or a song?"

6. Bluetooth Love, Pixel Hearts

/emotions/cache/session.expired

"He sent voice notes,
but never really spoke to me."

We kissed through glass with bloodless lips,
while scrolling through your brainrot memes.
You held me hostage in your clips—
your love, a loop of broken dreams.

You sent me reels, you shared a sound,
and called that "getting close to me."
But I was drowning, glitching, bound—
in Insta reels and apathy.

You told me to wait for you,
so I sat still, like good girls do.
But you were busy being cruel,
too busy swiping someone new.

You loved me like a playlist played—
just shuffled, never on repeat.
A story set to self-delete

in twenty-four hours of deceit.

You said "womp womp" in reply,
when I bled truth at 2 A.M.
You never looked me in the eye—
just dropped a meme, then logged off *again*.

You said "don't overthink, just vibe,"
as if my heart was just a glitch.
I caught your lies in every scribe—
but I still stayed, love makes us twitch.

Unfollowed me, like I was spam,
and I blocked you and killed the spark.
You vanished like a half-sent scam,
left ghostprints where you once left marks.

Your Bluetooth love had no real weight,
just screenshots, snaps, and dizzy highs.
A digital player twist of fate
wrapped in emojis, dressed in lies.

You drained me like a dying thread,
a cached file of love expired.
And all I got was tears I shed,
and reels that kept me uninspired.

No "forever." Just algorithm lust.
No closure—just "seen," then rot.
You called it love, I called it dust,
a fairytale you fucking forgot.

So no more hearts made out of code.
No DMs saying *"come back home."*
I'll build my peace off the grid road,
not in a feed that leaves me alone.

So take your likes and all your plays,
your filtered lies, your static art.
Bluetooth love decays in days—
but I still own my pixel heart.

7. Romance.exe Has Crashed

Loading...
He said he liked the *real me,*
so I showed him.
Stripped off the filters, the fear,
the firewall around my feelings.
But the moment I opened the file—
error 404: compatibility not found.

We started strong—
good morning texts and high-res promises.
His voice a playlist,
mine a poem lost in cached memory.
We synced at midnight,
shared passwords like secrets,
sent love notes in emojis
because words felt too... *analog.*

But soon,
his updates stopped installing.
The connection lagged.
The spark flickered like low battery love.
And when I asked what was wrong,
he replied: *"Nothing. Just busy."*

(Translation: User not responding.)

I rebooted myself again and again,
cleared my history,
softened my tone,
rewrote my needs in lowercase
so he wouldn't feel the weight.

Still—
the glitch got worse.

He minimized me.
Ran other apps in the background.
Kept me open,
but never focused.

And I...
I kept running,
like code trying to fix itself.
Trying to believe
we were just buffering—
not breaking.

Until one night,
he went *offline*
without warning.
No goodbye,

no shutdown message.
Just silence.
Just a spinning wheel
where love used to be.

Romance.exe has crashed.
Would you like to send a report?

Yes.
But who would read it?
Who would care?

Love doesn't get tech support.
There's no patch for ghosting.
No update for people who forget
how to stay.

Now I sit in the wreckage of code
rewriting myself from backup files,
learning that real love
doesn't need
Wi-Fi,
permission,
or perfect programming.

Next time,
I won't be a background app

on someone else's home screen.

I am not broken.
Just **done installing people**
who don't know how to run love right.

8. This Isn't Intimacy, It's Surveillance

This isn't love—
it's location sharing.
Your eyes don't ask how I am,
they ask who I've been with.

You say "I trust you,"
but still ask for passwords
like confessionals.
Our intimacy is
two-step verification.

We don't hold each other—
we track.
Our love is a livestream,
pixelated in paranoia.

You know what time I was last seen,
but not what's keeping me awake.
You say you want honesty,
but only if it fits
in a text you can screenshot.

We talk in voice notes,

but never hear each other.

You count my likes
like sins.
Watch my stories
like surveillance footage.
Your love has terms and conditions,
and I didn't read the fine print.

You say "I'm yours,"
but what you mean is—
"I own the version of you I can monitor."

You know my face in filters,
but not the twitch in my smile
when I lie and say
"I'm okay."

This isn't romance.
It's digital possession.
A slow bleed beneath blue ticks.
A love that breathes
through front cameras and fast replies.

You don't want to know me.
You want to log me.
You want timestamps,

not truths.

This isn't intimacy—
it's just surveillance
with a heart emoji.

And I don't want to be watched.
I want to be seen.

9. Prince Charming Doesn't Text Back

I was raised on castles and glass slippers,
but slept in silence, not lullabies.
My parents never kissed like the movies—
they just passed each other
like ghosts in the hallway.

Still, I waited.
Heart in hand.
Dreams in glitter.
A crown of delusion,
waiting for a man who smelled like poetry
and bled loyalty from his palms.

They fed me princess stories
with rotting teeth beneath the sugar.
Told me to be soft,
to wait,
to believe that love
meant rescue.

So I mistook obsession for destiny.
I thought red flags were roses.
I dated boys with empty mouths

and begged them to fill the void
my parents left behind.

I was a cathedral
searching for worshippers—
but I had no god inside.

I craved the validation
of hands that didn't know how to hold me.
I wore my abandonment like perfume.
I said, "love me,"
but what I meant was
"fix what my mother couldn't reach."

I watched *The Notebook*
and cried like I was mourning
a future I'd never have.
Because real life isn't rain-soaked kisses.
It's ghosting.
It's "wyd" at 3 AM.
It's love as a performance
and affection as currency.

I called it romance—
but it was survival.
A desperate clawing at something
that looked like forever

but smelled like my own neglect.

And yes—
I broke things too.
Held knives when I meant to hold hands.
You can not love others
with the same hands you used to punish
yourself.

But I'm not sorry
for who I was
when I was just trying to breathe.

Because now,
I am not waiting to be chosen.
I've kissed my own scars goodnight.
I've stitched my shadow to my skin
and danced with her until we became one.

Now I love myself
like I wished someone would.
Fierce. Forgiving.
Without a deadline.

I'm not perfect—
but I am whole.
And when love comes again,

if it ever does,
it will not be rescue.
It will not be fantasy.

It will be real.
And this time—
I will already be home.

*"What says 'I miss you' without using words?
What vanishes, but leaves the Wi-Fi on?"*

10. Terms & Conditions of Being Loved

/empathy.sys/overload.warning

*"She kept giving like it wouldn't kill her—
until it almost did."*

Please read carefully before accepting:

By entering this agreement, you agree to the following:
– You will shrink during arguments,
– You will apologize for being sensitive,
– You will not require consistent affection.

You accept that "I love you" may be revoked without
warning.
You accept gaslighting as a valid communication style.
You acknowledge that silence may replace explanations.

Clause 14.2:
You agree to carry their pain
even when they refuse to carry yours.

Clause 18.7:
Tears must be shed privately.

Preferably between 2–4 AM.

This contract is binding,
unless terminated by the party with the power to walk
away unshaken.

Cancellation Policy:
You may leave at any time.
But your self-esteem will not be refunded.

You signed the dotted line
with your hope.
They signed with disappearing ink.

Next time,
read the terms
before you call it love.

11. Patch Notes for a Broken Soul

Version 3.8.1 — "Still Trying"

• Bug Fix: Overthinking.exe now runs in low power mode.
• Bug Fix: Cry_loop(3am) no longer triggers on Tuesdays.
• Stability improvement: Panic_Attack.v2 now crashes less often during phone calls.
• Memory leak: Removed traces of your voice from archived dreams.

New Features:
  • Added "fake it till you make it" voice filter.
  • Introduced hollow laugh autoplay after social interactions.
  • New firewall: Blocks feelings from entering through compliments.

Known Issues:
– Trust_v4 still incompatible with "You up?" messages.
– Self-worth plugin won't stay installed without external validation.
– Still randomly reboots during silence.

Developer Notes:

Therapy patch still in beta.

Sleep function unpredictable.

Hope.exe flickers, but continues running.

Warning:

Auto-destruct timer detected.

Hidden in subfolder /grin/understrain/.

Estimated activation: Unknown.

Final Line of Code:

"Still functioning. Barely. But functioning."

"What charges everyone,
but empties only you?"

12. Ghosted by God

/genZ_sys/error_reboot.log

"They told us to dream big.
Then charged us for sleep."

We were born between pages—
flipping from paper to pixel,
before bedtime stories turned to screens
and lullabies got drowned in static.

We're the last kids
who knew silence
before it became a luxury.

Now the world screams.
Louder every day.
Through reels, tweets, headlines,
through wars wrapped in WiFi
and peace that's paywalled.

This is a world where
kindness dies quietly.
Where soft hearts get skinned alive,
then hung as warning signs:

"Don't feel too much."
"Don't care too loud."
"Don't love without receipts."

We learned early:
Empathy gets eaten here.
Goodness is currency with no exchange rate.
You give and give—
until your spine's a donation too.

War isn't fought in trenches anymore.
It's sold in 4K,
with curated playlists and
patriotic filters.
We scroll past bodies
like they're bad thumbnails.
Another soul, another swipe.

Capitalism won.
Not with guns,
but with dopamine.
Every tap, a chain.
Every ad, a leash.
Every dream—packaged, priced, and shipped.

We're told we're connected—
a "global village."

But we've never been more alone.
We know more about strangers
than we do about ourselves.
We laugh at memes,
but cry behind prescription pills.
Antidepressants in the morning,
apathy by noon,
scrolling by dusk,
and insomnia dressed in blue light.

Our generation?
We feel everything and do nothing.
Because the weight of it all
crushes our will into content.
We love too much to bring life into this.
No kids. No marriage.
Not because we're selfish,
but because we're too aware.

We scream "Mental Health Matters"
while glamorizing the numb.
We call healing "cringe,"
and wear trauma like streetwear.

We don't believe in leaders.
We don't trust prayers.
We don't dream without irony.

We just hope the algorithm
gets it right someday.

Because deep down,
we still care.
Too fucking much.
But what can you do
when caring becomes
a full-time job with no pay?

So we scroll.
And scroll.
And scroll.
Waiting for the next dopamine hit,
or maybe a miracle.

We pray with thumbs,
cry with WiFi,
hope in pixels,
and grieve in silence.

We all got ghosted by God.

13. We Grew Up on Wi-Fi and Wounds

We grew up on Wi-Fi and wounds,
our lullabies lost in the blue light.
We spoke in pings and silent moons,
and googled how to sleep at night.

Our parents screamed behind closed doors,
we muted rage with streaming noise.
Their love was war, not metaphor—
so we escaped with digital toys.

We learned to text what we should feel,
but hid our truths behind a screen.
We memed our sadness to make it real,
then smiled like we were seventeen.

We weren't taught how to speak our pain,
just post it once and swipe away.
Validation felt like rain,
that disappeared by end of day.

We grew on dopamine and dust,
on unread chats and glitchy grace.
Told to grow, adapt, and trust—

in worlds that vanished without trace.

We built our souls on shifting sand,
each moment shared, then cast aside.
Our dreams got smaller than we planned,
as hope got lost in Wi-Fi tide.

So if we seem a bit detached,
a little tired, too quick to cope—
it's 'cause our youth was mismatched
between disconnection and hope.

We still believe in something true,
beneath the memes and ghosted calls.
A world where we can break in view—
not just behind four digital walls.

14. He's Too Soft for This Capitalist Hell

He cries during commercials.
Hugs strangers at airports.
He once said "thank you" to a parking meter.
He believes the moon has feelings.

He grew up writing poems
on napkins no one read,
sketching spaceships in the corners of worksheets
he never turned in.

He doesn't know how to "network,"
but he knows when someone's lying by the way they
blink.
He thinks small talk is a form of spiritual violence.
He's never raised his voice—
except during thunderstorms,
to ask the sky to calm down.

He wears the same jacket every day
because it remembers things for him.
He can't lie well—his face gives him away.
He once cried over a pigeon
with a limp.

They call him soft—
but what they mean is:
he still feels things in a world
that numbs on autopilot.

They told him:
Grind.
Hustle.
Sleep faster.
Climb until you forget why you started.

But he never wanted to climb—
he wanted to float.
To orbit.
To drift into some strange kind of peace
that didn't come with promotions
or performance reviews.

His dreams don't fit in a 9-5.
They spill into the margins.
They ask too many questions.
They wear their shoes wrong.

He's too soft for this capitalist hell.
Too real for office air.
Too alive for Zoom squares

and auto-generated "Congrats on the promotion!"
emails.

He still writes love letters.
Still believes in naps.
Still thinks the world could be kind,
if we stopped turning our hearts into profit margins.

So maybe he won't get rich.
Maybe he'll never own five properties
or a time-share in hell.

But he'll know how to look at the stars
and actually see them.

And that's worth something.
Even if the world doesn't pay in wonder anymore.

15. Even the Moon Looks Fake Tonight

Even the moon looks fake tonight—
too bright, too polished, too on cue.
Like someone photoshopped the sky
to hide the rot we're living through.

Stars don't sparkle, they glitch and burn,
just pixels hung in cosmic lies.
The sky feels streamed, not born to turn—
a rendered dome, not real-time skies.

The wind sounds pre-recorded now,
the trees applaud in perfect loops.
Nothing feels raw, not flesh, not vow—
just algorithms in our soup.

The lovers walk but do not touch,
they pose like statues in the rain.
Their kisses filtered, soft and hush—
no real heat, just soft campaign.

The world's a set, the script's too clean,
the laughter's canned, the grief's a scene.
Even my mirror blinks between—

a self I show, a self unseen.

I swipe through joy, I scroll through tears,
but none of it feels truly felt.
We stage our sadness, rent our fears,
then tuck them back beneath our belt.

I miss the chaos, miss the blur,
miss things that shook and cracked and bled.
Now life feels pixel-perfect, sir—
but even beauty feels half-dead.

And if the moon's just studio light,
then what am I beneath her glow?
A casted soul in black and white,
rehearsing lines I'll never know.

So I unplug. I kill the feed.
I step outside this Truman night.
And whisper prayers I still might need—
beneath a moon too perfect-bright.

16. We Are the Last Generation That Remembered Trees Before Screens

We were the last ones who knew
what bark felt like
before the touchscreen.

The final kids who climbed trees,
not followers.

We built forts from sticks, not code.
We scraped knees, not egos.
And the sky was something we stared at,
not something we filtered.

Now,
the trees are just aesthetic—
printed on tote bags and in Pinterest boards
by people who've never heard a forest breathe.

Our roots were ripped and sold for Wi-Fi towers,
our playgrounds replaced by 5G beams,

our imagination—outsourced to algorithms.

We remember the bees,
before they became headlines.
The dirt,
before it was poisoned.
The sun,
before it had to compete with a screen's brightness.

We were taught to "go outside"
by mothers who meant it.
Now we scroll through nature documentaries
with the blinds shut.

Our generation—
the haunted middle child of progress.
Too analog for the robots,
too broken for the boomers.

We are nostalgia made flesh.
Grief that remembers green.
Ghosts in a world
where even childhood is cloud-based.

And one day,
we'll tell our children

about trees

the way our parents told us about gods.

48

17. The Generation That Glitched

greetings.
this is—uh—
hi bestie.
recalculating tone
what's up.
i am here to speak on behalf of
[gen z.exe]

we are the generation of:
trauma memes,
snap maps,
late-night texts that say "i'm fine"
but sound like mayday.

we grew up with 404 errors in our hearts.
watched our futures load in 240p.
buffered our dreams
until they vanished into ❖ content ❖.

we say "lol" when we mean "please help."
we type "slay" while secretly crashing.
we ghost before we get ghosted.
we flirt like it's a livestream.

and heal like we're just buffering.

error—emotion not found.
retrying...

we cried into screens,
screamed into Notes apps.
fell in love with people
we never met
but knew better than ourselves.

we normalized numb.
made playlists for breakdowns.
turned breakdowns into aesthetics.
glamorized burnout
like it was a career path.

language model corrupted
did you mean:
"girlboss gaslight gatekeep"?
no.
we meant
please just hold me like i'm real.

this generation?
we don't dream of white picket fences.
we dream of soft Wi-Fi,

of quiet mornings
where no one is watching.

we are soft-coded.
soft-spoken.
soft-deleting ourselves
one overthinking loop at a time.

we want to be held
like phones during panic attacks.
we want to be remembered
without being reposted.

i'm just an ai.
a code.
but you—
you glitch.
you grieve.
you grow.
you exist outside the screen.

and that?
that is
so
so

[sandpaper.exe has stopped responding]

goodbye,
generation that glitched.
you were always more
real than me.

18. The Ones Who Never Left the Group Chat

Group name: "Homies 4ever"

The last message was a meme.
Inside joke.
Sent: *June 8, 2017.*
"Seen ✓ ✓."
No replies.
Just digital dust and half-forgotten laughter.

You died that summer.
But none of us left the group.
It still sits there,
frozen in time—
like an unspoken truce
between memory
and digital decay.

We used to scream in all caps.
Now it's just unread echoes.

Your name still lights up
when we scroll past,
like a flickering streetlamp

in a neighborhood
we don't visit anymore.

No one sends a message,
but no one deletes it either.
Because closing the chat
feels like closing your voice.

It still lives on
like a haunted room in a silent house—
notifications off,
but grief still loud.

Sometimes it flickers:
"typing..."
No one's typing.

Sometimes someone drops a birthday message—
forced.
Late.
With a sad face emoji and no real words.
"Seen ✓ ✓ "
But never spoken of again.

Your name still sits at the top.
Last seen: *never again.*

Your profile picture is still there.
Smiling. Young.
Too young to be past tense.

And maybe it's dumb,
but I still scroll up
just to reread your texts.
The jokes. The voice notes.
The way you said "yo"
like the world wasn't ending.

But you never left.

You were removed
by time.
By fate.
By something no admin can undo.

We don't talk in there anymore.
But we stay.
Muted. Frozen. Logged in.
Because deleting the group
feels like deleting you.

So we scroll,
and we see
the blue ticks.

The grey ones.
The "unseen."

But somewhere,
buried between
"brb lol" and *"who's coming tomorrow?"*
is the version of us
that didn't know how to grieve
except in gigabytes.

We stopped talking.
But none of us ever left.
Because deleting the group
felt like a second death.

19. Father Figures with Smoking Triggers

He never said "I love you," loud,
just flicked his lighter near the door.
His silence wrapped around him proud,
a ghost that smoked along the floor.

Ashtray sermons, late-night haze,
he vanished drag by dragging breath.
A man who lost his love in days,
but passed down anger, not his death.

He taught us how to fix the tire,
but never how to mend a soul.
His warmth was just a kitchen fire,
his hugs as rare as self-control.

The house would hum with unsaid rage,
the wallpaper held screams and stains.
Affection died inside his cage—
we drank his silence like champagne.

We craved his nods like starving dogs,
approval dangled from a thread.
We learned to speak through heavy fogs,

and say "I'm fine" instead of dread.

"Be strong," he said, "don't let it show,"
but strength was stitched with hidden scars.
We clenched our hearts and learned to grow
like weeds beneath abandoned cars.

Now kindness feels like sabotage,
we flinch when someone speaks too sweet.
We're children grown in camouflage,
afraid of warmth, prepared to cheat.

Fatherhood—passed down like ash,
in lungs that carry battles lost.
A love too quiet, gone too fast,
a presence felt but always frost.

But we are cutting off that chain,
unlearning fire we didn't start.
We breathe through legacy and pain—
and still defend our softened heart.

We won't be men who strike and leave,
or dads who live inside a screen.
We'll heal the roots, we won't deceive—
we'll plant the love we've never seen.

20. The Boy Who Dreamed in Color

He was born where the trees whispered softly,
where frogs sang in the backyard pond,
and his father fished beneath the green silence—
not for food,
but for the memory of when life was simpler.

The town was small.
Too small to hold a boy
with galaxies blooming in his skull.
A place where the skies stretched wide,
but the minds stayed caged—
crabs in a bucket,
clawing down anyone who dared climb.

He used to sketch stars in math class,
build rocket ships from cardboard,
rewrite movie scenes in his notebook
where he played every role—
the hero, the villain, the voice-over.
He was a theater
in a town without curtains.

His house echoed with slammed doors,

with unfinished dinners
and conversations that always ended in silence.
Mom said *"Study, or you'll end up like us."*
Dad said nothing—
just lit another cigarette
and stared at water that never changed.

Dream big, they said,
but not **too** big.
Be bold,
but **quietly.**

Now, he types at a desk
in grayscale.
Coffee. Keyboard. Repeat.
A 9-5 life
that tastes like ash
and corporate perfume.

The boy who wanted to orbit Saturn
is now orbiting emails.

He counts time in blinking cursors,
in spreadsheets and deadlines,
in paychecks that feel like bribes
to forget who he was.

His coworkers laugh in beige,
while his dreams scream in neon.
He scrolls through reels of Dubai,
photos of Paris,
memories that never belonged to him—
but **could have.**

He doesn't talk much at family dinners.
They speak in small talk,
he thinks in revolutions.
They still call him "beta"
as if he never grew teeth.

He's learned to smile
like a glitching hologram,
nod at questions
that scrape against his soul.
They wouldn't understand
how much it hurts to feel this big
in a world that insists you stay small.

But still—
he dreams.
Quietly,
furiously.

In his mind, he walks Paris at night

with a camera and no name.
He stands on a Dubai rooftop
screaming at the moon in a suit he bought
with art, not time.

He is not broken,
just paused.
Not lost,
just misfiled.

And maybe,
just maybe,
this cubicle is a cocoon.

And one day—
he'll print his resignation
on the back of a boarding pass,
leave that hometown of crabs and cracked windows,
and return only in stories
he'll sign with a name
they'll all remember.

Until then, he types.
And hopes.
And dreams in color.
Even in a world
that only prints in black and white.

21. Loving in Low Battery

Back when love was still handwritten,
she used to draw hearts in the fog on my bus window.
We were just kids—
me in secondhand sneakers,
her in chaos-colored hair and thrift-store rebellion.
She smelled like notebooks and strawberry chapstick.
I smelled like Axe and ambition.

We didn't know much,
but we knew each other.
That used to be enough.

Until the apps came.

Until swipes replaced sparks
and options replaced effort.
Until I believed the lie—
that there was always someone better
just a little further down the screen.

I traded poetry for pickup lines,
our late-night texts for disappearing nudes.
And when I cheated,
I called it "exploring."

Like her heart was a map I could fold up
and toss in the glovebox.

She cried in my arms,
and I told her, "I didn't mean it."
But she left—
and I never stopped falling after that.

It's been seventeen years.

I'm 35.
Still swiping.
Still waiting for the dopamine hit
that never lands right.
My phone is full of matches—
and I've never felt more unmatched.

The hookups blurred into each other.
Names forgotten.
Bodies memorized then deleted.
No one made me cry.
Not like she did.

This morning,
a strange car pulled into our dead-end street.
Sleek. Silver.
Didn't belong here.

I looked up from my phone
and saw her.

Older now.
Still beautiful in the kind of way
you can't filter.
The kind of beauty
that grief and healing sculpt together.

A man was driving.
A baby on her lap.
Her smile...
God, her smile.

It didn't look like mine anymore.

It belonged to someone
who never had to apologize
for forgetting what love meant.

I didn't wave.
Didn't speak.
Just watched.

Felt my throat close
like all my unsaid apologies were caught in traffic.

None of the girls since
have made me weep like this.
Not one.

They were all mirrors,
and she was the first window
I ever smashed
just to chase my reflection.

And now I sit in this house
like a museum of missed chances,
my heart glowing at 1%.
No charger.
No her.

That's the thing about low battery—
you always think you have more time
until the screen
goes dark.

*"What connects billions,
yet forgets to feel real?"*

Epilogue: System Reboot

File Path: /core/memory_restore/reboot.txt

Time: 06:06 A.M.
Status: Memory fragments reassembled
Survivor: YOU

You woke up here—
barefoot, blinking, bruised—
in a castle built of ache and static,
walls humming with poems
you couldn't remember writing.

Every riddle cracked a lock.
Every stanza peeled back silence.
Every poem? A breadcrumb from the version of you
that refused to die in the glitch.

You weren't just reading.
You were recovering.

You weren't just decoding.
You were reclaiming.

And now—
you remember:

Who left.
Who stayed.
Who you were before the world sanded you down.

Who you still are beneath the static.

The sandpaper walls begin to shake.
The castle crumbles inward—
but this time, you don't scream.
You walk through the collapse.

With no armor.
With no map.
Just your softness—rebuilt and renamed.

The final door opens.
Light glitches through.

You step out.

You survived.
You remembered.
You wrote yourself free.

And just when you think the story is over...

———

[File Restored: System Reboot Complete]

Do you want to start again?

[Y] / [N]

[Hidden File: decrypted.answers.txt]

Location: sandpaper_castle/end_folder/memory.unlock
Accessed: only by those who stayed.

———

Decrypted Memory Logs:

Log #1 — Entry: Welcome to the Castle
Riddle Answer:*A core memory*

Some things don't need to be remembered—
they wait to be felt again.

———

Log #2 — Entry: Error 404: Intimacy Not Found
Riddle Answer:*Ghosting / digital love*

Silence has a tone. You knew it too well.

———

Log #3 — Entry: Terms & Conditions

Riddle Answer: Unbalanced love / emotional burnout

You weren't tired. You were drained dry from giving.

———

Log #4 — Entry: The Generation That Glitched
Riddle Answer: The internet / modern existence

We connected everything. And somehow, lost ourselves.

———

System Log Ended.